These Are Not My Words

I Just Wrote Them

These Are Not My Words

I Just Wrote Them

DONOVAN HUFNAGLE

RESOURCE *Publications* · Eugene, Oregon

THESE ARE NOT MY WORDS
I Just Wrote Them

Resource Publications
An Imprint of Wipf and Stock Publishers
199 W. 8th Ave., Suite 3
Eugene, OR 97401

www.wipfandstock.com

PAPERBACK ISBN: 979-8-3852-2399-2
HARDCOVER ISBN: 979-8-3852-2400-5
EBOOK ISBN: 979-8-3852-2401-2

Thank you to my family, my friends, my mentors,
and my students

"I've tried to become someone else for a while, only to discover that he, too, was me."—STEPHEN DUNN

Contents

CONTENTS

Thank you to the journals that helped these words reach more people along the way:

The Closed Eye Open
"Secret Identity"

Moonstone Press
"Sussudio Saves, the Day After, #6"

Sojourn
"Heroic Code:"

Sojourn
"…at home" published as "Doppelganger"
"www.blues.com."

Poetry Society of New Hampshire
"Bar Girl"

The Northridge Review
"86 the Mustard"

The New York Quarterly
"Hobo Henry"

"GREEK STUDY—PENSACOLA FLORIDA" OR FIRST GREEK

Christ was sitting on an old empty orange crate
eating grapes and enjoying the morning breeze
when he spoke of the old country's state:

Greeks live a life of the average American gait.
Some farm, but the majority make a living on the seas,
while Christ sits on an old empty orange crate.

At 85 he still had a good memory to date,
and, I thought, he may well be the oldest Greek
in Pensacola as he spoke of the old country's state.

His eyes glistened mining about his fate,
moving to New York in 1883 from Saloniki, Greece.
While Christ sits on an old empty orange crate,

he recalled the old street cars, sidewalks made
of planks, and the Florida sandy streets
after he spoke of the old country's state.

He has great admiration for his adopted home state.
Sun withered; he will spend the rest of life with his buddies.
And Christ sits on an old empty orange crate,
speaking of the old country's state.

CREDENTIALS

for my wife

Lenny sang, *I am you, you are...*

I am
a scrapbook of personas and craft,
construction paper and paint pens,
a collage of memories and unicorn stickers,
a cut out of souls and pasted hearts all
from those that have witnessed and been
witnessed, those that have taught me.

I am
a collective of everyone and everyone's
collective.

I am mi abuelita stirring pinto beans, lost in Los
Panchos. I see her costume jewelry ribboned around
her neck. Red. Her lips red. Her cheeks rosy. White band
wraps her black curls. She stirs. She tastes.

I am "just a bit more salt."

I am mi abuelito, Grandpa Tony. I know polyester slacks and
salt and peppered slicks across my head. I know his bologna and
white bread. Oaxaca discs like tortillas.

I am the spirits of each and all—They.

I am Mother: outfit for every occasion.
    Planned. Prepared. Patience.

2

I am Father: outfit for every occasion.
 Independent. Able. Critical.
                    I found my tears after he beat me for holding my
eighth-grade
boyfriend's hand. I found new clothes when Mama took me shop-
ping.

I am my husband.
I am friends. Curdled milk—an experiment
        of firm and fluidity.

I am my children—the stick
legs and arms, two bubbles holding my circle chin
beneath the crayon tree. I hold your hand.

I am your feet dangling
in the air mid-cartwheel.

I am the toys under the water's skin. Dive.
I am the heart praying before the fall. Pedal.

I am "What's for dinner?"

I am
you and you
        are.

I am
a first impression (and a lasting one at that). The clothes that fit…

I am heel…
I am boot
I am Jordans
I am glitter and fuzz

I am a hug. A kiss. A look of love.

I am the smirk of disappointment.

I am the uninvited ache,   after all,

I am human and will die one day.
How often I wake to my back screaming? Is it
the mattress? The pillow? My chest? Is it
the untold narrative combating the cracks in memory.

I am
not the man who fucked my childhood
with his hand.

I am that man, too

I am joy,   after all,

I am human and am alive today.
How often I fall to the husband…fall in love like sleep.

I am the questions within the answers stated
as questions.

I am "those are not my words; I just wrote them."

I am Hook, Wendy ever chasing after the elusive flying boy.

I am The Labyrinth, the baby brother captured by the goblin king.

I am the sleeping panther *undisturbed by the rush of men,*
the sum of women,   *the hum of trade.* Fort Worth.

I am the tajin barnacled, ringing the rim of my Bloody Mary.

I am
what I eat.

I am   the morning;
I enter today's race on snooze.

I am "ask me after my coffee."

I am the sparkle of time
that moment of realization,
the time of recollection,
the time it takes to shake my right
hand, remembering left is not right
and right is not left.

I am "go that way."

I am Hola
I am Hello
I am the duality of (wo)man.

YOIU

Why do I always put i
in you? I blame it on
dyslexia but it could be Id.

It could be my flying fingers.
Like flags of lip and cheek
flapping from a Bassett Hound's
jaw—my fingers fumble without
the proper arch over the keys. First
the ring finger followed by the middle
and then the pointer. Each one
in sequence stumble in a row
like a chain gang. Clink, Clink,

Clink. Will this sentence ever end?

It could be sublimation. Perhaps the i
is I silenced. Just listen to the word;
can you hear me? The pronoun hushed,
muzzled by the others. Am I just a good
for nothing?

It could be that I am just fantasying,
and i dreams being
in you. Where's the foreplay,
the trace of your hand
dressing me down—your eyes
filling my ego?

It could be displacement. Can
I blame it on the dog, kick it? That *it*

"in which there is no I
or You."

I tried to put u before me, but
it could be that i always
comes before u and that still doesn't
get me anywhere. And I am
sorry for that.

I wonder what would happen if I
just crossed yoiu out.

I, POET

I learn to write from Jeffé Hidalgo,
 brother to Juan. We long hand on his rotgut
porch—a mixture of tequila, coffee,
and splintered pine wood.

The Havana smoke—like bloodlines,
like rivers into springs, into gulfs, like figments
of imagination, filter into puddles onto paper.
He is me and I am him.

And we face the swamp while stray
dogs and flies clash for flesh. Hounds nip at their wings,
wisps of translucent dreams. Flies
swarm while hounds scream and whine.

and we listen
to Rafael Méndez scratch
the record player

and we hear
the rocking of his chair creek;
it calls to the echoes

and we wait
for a response. And we wait
for a response. We wait.

He taught me everything he knows
except for the things he doesn't want me to know.
He saves the unknown, the untold,
the intangible and his most intimate visions.

He shares those in his poetry.

He once wrote about his *gato* curling
beneath his rocking, but he didn't even have a cat.
And just like me, the cat became a dog
or whatever the clouds shape

in the moment of that day.

LOST AND FOUND

Charles handles his last draw of whiskey. Leigh
lights up and like a dragon's tail, he drags
the smoke with him from inside out. Joseph
always looks down and enters his reflection
every time he lifts his glass.

I'm bartending because I want to become
a writer and fashion language old, I pour simple
syrup sweet and dash bitters bit by bit—
to express, to feel the emptiness of a lowball.

This—more than ever—is a necessity.

I pour big—death and desire, epic and metaphor,
Flora and the country green, the end of one life path
over another and into a Nightingale.

And tiny dust, the articles that bind language,
skin and hair, mites and bite after bite
of pollen and poesy; they linger within the sunbeam.

And like snowflakes just hold out your tongue.
Contain the convulsive breathing and wait. Wait
for cough-like emotions to spasm and poetry to melt
away and dust to disappear.

Whiskey drags out in every glass, and I'm
reminded that I'm tender, a barkeep because
I'm a writer—a mutual acceptance—as John says,
another self-same song that found a path.

MINDSET

Sometimes I wish my mind was perforated,
memories easily torn away.

GRANDMA, IF ONLY THESE WALLS...

Do you sleep naked beneath
a popcorn sky riddled with residue
of the past and clues to asbestos?
I remember

when I clawed the ceiling,
the putty knife scraped away
the yellowing kernels and it snowed
for the rest of the day. For the rest
of my life.

They popped. And from the ceiling,
down, eventually,
yellow falls asleep on the bed.
I am a child in a snow globe,
making snow angels the same
yellowish tint as her nubs, her alley-cat
eyes, these walls.

I know little of her:
her modeling days—her costume
jewelry displays throughout
the house, but where did she wear this
ruby ring? When did this
emerald rest around her neck?
An albatross?

I imagine her strut
on the runway, such
power. They stare at her, wait
for her everything. A look. A twist.

A wink. Was she always on
display?

Did the flash of cameras blind her
marriage—rumors of others,
into another?

How the hell could she let
the next in? He stole her
money, molested her
children and grands. He smoldered her
like the tip of her cigarette,
And from the tip, down,
eventually, the ash snow fell
gray to yellow.

"FUR WORKERS" OR STRIKE ON 28TH STREET

"Why should I have to suffer so?"
He says, "I'm doing this because you're doing it;
I do the same thing the others do."

We come into the station house, they burrow
for my name. He asks, "How do you spell it?"
Why should I have to suffer so?

I was going to put up a fight and screw
with him. After all, they're supposed to protect,
but I do the same thing the others do.

So when I wanted to mow
something dirty, I'd say, "I know how to sign it."
Why should I have to suffer so?

"You are looking for a place to stab me blue."
The police asks again, "How do you spell it?"
I do the same thing the others do.

I try to tell about the Shoe shop on strike,
and we had a call—gangsters are all in it,
so why should I have to suffer so?
I do the same thing the others do.

STARS

Like our past it takes eight minutes
for the sun's shine to reach earth.
But they say that most of the stars
we see blink at us are already dead.

RITUAL

A pond—
and Father baits the hook.
A night crawler—
and mumbles of girls between men.
Between his past and my present.
I am man
now.

Tadpoles—
and fireflies.
Shadows and light—
A swim below and above the reflective
calm.
Blades of untamed reeds—
I Rise beyond.
Mud—
and spider webs.
Between Cottonwoods—
and I tell a tale of my first fish,
caught with my father,
at least,
that is the tale—
I like to tell.

ROLE MODEL

The salt and sea, the spit and anger outside
the harbor wages war against the intrusion
of (un)natural rock and sand. Insincere like a
mother's finger to a crying baby's lips,
"Shhh. it will be okay," like a tit in its mouth.

And do you know what would happen to that thirst
if it were to be denied?

And all the while, the yachts and dinghies
inside the harbor still and calm like gentlemen.
Manmade like *a father's interest...more than*
a son's indifference. They bob atop a silent storm,
hidden from and hiding for.

Gentlemen have to be very careful of what they *do.*

I want my son to know me, but I fear
I have only offered control, violence,
insensitivity, restriction, emotion   less.
Manmade like a jetty silencing spring and summer,
the fall. I fear winter is all he knows.

     Dear Son,

          Perhaps, someday, *after I am dead,*
          you may come to learn right from wrong
          of this and perhaps, one day, if I am gone,
          you will write the words that kill
          only to feel alive again like an epitaph
          in granite.

MY STEP

Grandfather's eyes follow his hands
snaking into my closet. Molested
as a child, I cannot find my humanity.
My m_mori_s lay like a half-filled cross-
word puzzle. Two down. One across.

And now, as a man, I fuck as a child.

I paw flesh like an action figure: GI Joe
on top of Barbie on Christmas morning.
Plastic hump against plastic hump. Don't
girls have a vagina and boys a penis?

She doesn't have areoles or nipples, either.

One morning I opened my parent's bedroom
without knocking. I only needed toothpaste.
I have never seen like that—Mom's breasts—
the pink against flesh, the erect against soft.
        I didn't know any better. Plastic is all I knew.

*By the power of Grayskull (*and my parents), I have:

He-Man (Prince Adam), Skeletor,

Orko, Battle-Cat (Cringer),

Man-at-Arms, Beast man,

Trap-Jaw, and Teela.

She-Ra came later.

The transition fumes exhausted from Joe
to He, gun to sword, tank to tiger, Cobra
Commander to Skeletor. Prince Adam holds
up his sword, yells, and births man—a He-
Man. By the way, I learned early on that if
you don't carry a chiseled chest—a shelf
for crumbs to gather—high-top shoulders,
a pack of six or eight, tubes streaking down
your biceps, yoiu are not He or Man.

Teela, Battle-Ram's daughter, wants to fuck
He-Man. Well, He-Man wants to fuck Teela
if I'm being honest. She-Ra turns out to be
his twin sister.

      Kathleen, we call her Beanie since
she loves green beans, toured the scene
with my younger sister. Best friends.
      I didn't really see her until I saw, well,
her She-Ra. At one point I was playing
hide and seek. Years later I wanted
to play *hide and seek* with her.

In the beginning was the Word, and the
Word was with God, and the Word was
Star Wars. For a young boy, Luke was God.
Forget GI Joe and He-Man. Forget Cobra
Commander and Skeletor, there was Darth
Vader. If only I kept my Luke and Vader.
What would they be worth today? If a child

preserves toys as jams, are they truly a child
anymore? Anyway, when they kiss,

both Leia and Luke feel the force. It takes
a lifetime to recover.

I married after three engagements.
Divorced after one. Remarried. Plastic
roleplay recycled. Divorced. Remarried
again. Plastic made to be remade.
I didn't know any better.

Plastic is all I know.

FIRST LOVES

It is one day before my 50th and what was important
to me yesterday seems more today.

I traveled back to my home on Alvarez. A place
I have not felt in years. Loves like monuments:

Lauren lives across from me.
Her house holds two second-
story eyes, windows that stare
into an empty cul-de-sac, a street
lamp glows above her mailbox.

Her older sisters, Jenny and
Michael (like a boy named
Sue), occupy the left and the right
eye, respectfully. Lauren's room
lingers in the home's mind
behind her sisters' vision. Does
she dream of me? I dream of her.
I love her as much as a thirteen-
year-old boy can love.

Jenny would wink at times,
the light of her room filtering
through the open miniblinds.
It's time for bed, and I would
hope like a whining dog, panting,
fogging the glass door, waiting
to be let outside. I would watch
until she closes her eye
for the evening. Although, I never

reach that moment, the flash
of skin, breast or other before
the light is blinded and blocked.

Lauren occasionally sits my younger
sister. Normally, we stay home, and
she boils the water for our *mac n
chee*, microwaves Oscar Meyers
to tag along. This time, we stay
at her house. From the entrance,
under the stairs lives a wooden
cabinet—32"H X 16"W X 6'L. Lauren
lifts the top, exposing a record
player. She switches some switches,
the lever spills on the spinning
record, and Al Jolson spouts,
out—

> *There's a rainbow around my shoulder*
> *And a sky of blue above*
> *Oh the sun shines bright, the world's all right*
> *'Cause I'm in love*

We dance and sing. We spin like
the record. We spin like "Ring Around
a Rosies." We spin and curtsy, spin
and *all fall down*. When we fall,
isn't it always down? I think to myself.
When we think, isn't it always to
yourself? Anyway, *Ashes! Ashes!*

Lauren, her two sisters, and her mom
live alone. All women. The secret to
hiding as a man is to wipe the toilet
ring and lower the seat. I piss as well
as any thirteen-year-old boy can piss.

Lauren's mom asks me to wipe some
more. "We sit, you stand." She repeats,
pointing at the base of the toilet. "We
sit, you stand."

Kevin lives two houses down from
Lauren. His younger sister, Kathleen,
(mentioned in a previous poem)
stays best friends with my sister until
they turn…like all best friends do. Well,
maybe not all best friends, but in
this case, they both fall ~~down~~. I
can't go into too many details,
since we are entering into my
sister's poem, but from what math
I know: B = Boyfriend; T = Time;
F = Fiancée; H = Husband; and D =
Death to Friendship.

If B + T = F and F + T = H then
H + T = D.

Kevin has an older sister, too.
David wants Kim. Does Kim want
David?

I look up to Kevin even though
we only stand a year apart. I
wear a similar purple and pink
plaid sweater vest. He rides a
Diamond Back. I have a Huffy
knockoff. He skates on a Tony
Hawk. I have a board, too. My
first skateboard gleams white
with black grip tape. Pink rails,

skid pad, and wheels. My last
skateboard was a burnt orange
Lucero three.

Launch ramps consume most
of our summer. The higher we
rise, the longer we drift. With each
launch, Kevin climbs.

David, though, was my idol.
Older, longer hair, picture Turtle
in the movie North Shore.

      I don't know about Kim, even though
David shared the time they went surfing,
and she gripped her neoprene, shedding
her surf skin into shorts in front of him.
50 shades? Or dreams of an 18-year-old?

But Shelly and Shannon, a few years younger
than David, held an infatuation for him,
an idol for us three. If Shannon's locks
flowed the length of Rapunzel, she would
have laddered from her window. Her father
held her in her room most days.

Shelly flashed us from hers.

      I scan the TV channels for snow
and wait for flashes of skin and fuzz.
I picture each in the furry of the blizzard.

      Why do I carry these carnival mirror
perspectives?
Are they narratives bloated from myth and dreams?

Or

dreams from truths? I can't seem to tell anymore.

"BIG TONY" OR THOSE GIRLS

Those girls up at Reliable's were funny as hell.
Ask them, darn near any one of them, where'd they work.
They didn't want anybody to know; they didn't tell.

"Oh, I'm the switchboard operator," they'd say. "I dwell
in the office." Ashamed, see. Fibbed like clockwork.
Those girls up at Reliable's were funny as hell.

Say, they'd even ring their boyfriends the sound of that bell.
All those dumb dames putting on an act, shoveling that murk.
They didn't want anybody to know; they didn't tell.

When the girls come out, Big Tony wisecracked about the swell
switchboard operators. They put their foot in it, so they just
smirked.
Those girls up at Reliable's were funny as hell.

He hung around with his gang; they were in on it as well.
When the girls come out, they talked real loud like fireworks.
They didn't want anybody to know; they didn't tell.

Tony laid it on thick! How he laid it on well!
He pretending he didn't know the girls was lurking.
Those girls up at Reliable's were funny as hell.
Why they didn't want anybody to know, they wouldn't tell.

LAID TO REST

Have you seen the exhibit,
a series of photographs? It
felt like Christmas:

a humbled substance, laid
beneath feet, nurtured, replenished,
protected. Ancient and pleasantly
coarse.

This filth is valuable. This filth
is essential. Eroded
and crumbled.

Sometimes I wish they hadn't been
published as an appendix, classified as useless
and dangerous without objection.

Have you seen the dam of a once
deep river, a deep river behind us,
drained and filled with the bones
of my mother and father? "Oh! Mother,
the loss."

6.5 millimeter bolt action rifle
six-shot repeating rifle—
a hair trigger
2 pounds for a trigger pull.

the nature, the characteristics—
in war and in peace
these are the same.

A few thousands of an inch
formed the first line of battle.

The sun never rose
brighter than that Sunday
morning.

SECRET IDENTITY

Superman
uses Clark, shielded by vanity
glasses. Would sunglasses dim
his laser eyes burnt in by the sun?

Batman
hermits inside a cave. Plato
behind his father, his
wealth, chained by his shape.

The Invisible
Man tells tales of shadows—*how
shadows are the source of identity.*

But shadows are just simple shapes of
things—man and beast on walls carried
over from the light into darkness without.

Empty

and without soul or purpose, they follow
the past, reminiscence of what was once
ours, our humanity constantly chasing
the present but permanently behind. Or
haunting reminders to fight against the very
same walls that canvas our shadows.

The Hulk
becomes incredible, a beast-man within
a man, outside of himself no longer a man.
A game of Hyde and seek.

"Wonder Twin
powers activate!" Jayna forms an eagle.
Her brother just puddles through her claws.

Why not an albatross?

As if it had been a Christian soul...
born to fall and yet still fly...*We hailed it in
God's name.*

Prince Adam
has the power within, closeting all his glory
as He-man comes out. He waves his sword
about. I become a husband. I become a father.
I become a teacher. I become a writer, a man,
a feminist—I become...

I hide in front of these masks *simply because
people refuse to see me* without these masks.

HEROIC CODE:

surge and blunder through the mythic twilight
of time and space; conquer archenemies
like Joker, Luther, Zorak, Kitch Loren (?);
boast of victory, feast and song—*na na
na, gonna have a good time*—praise by all;
fame and glory only reached through action;
spoil the takeover of Ghost Planet
or win a love match between Blimp's over-
loaded *destructo-vac;*
Descent into
the underworld: the hornet's nest where time
dreams and masks yield secret identities.

A hero is eager to confront death—
the best in war, kill—in peace, family.
Does code permit choice? Lenience or lunacy?

...AT HOME.

The Brown Hornet, like Space Ghost,
possesses
no Wonderland. Black outer space is like
Shakespeare's green, a midsummer's night
forest
where heroes stay super and masks still hide,

where logic and reason withdraw. Judgement
and thought, like OZ, transpire in a dream.
The cosmos holds time by the woven seams—
seconds as hours, ages as mouse moments.

Cosby, thru Brown Hornet, snaps his finger.
And, in an instant, the junkyard gang woos.
Happy ending for Tweeterbell, Stinger,
and Hornet.
            From the unknown to the true

and above the outer, Bill says, *I wouldn't
advise any of you to attempt this...*

JOKER

"and that is why Jack Nicholas
is the best Joker."

He replies. "I grew up with 'Have you
ever danced with the devil in the pale
moon light?'"

He was the only one without
a painted face,

wipe away the makeup after
the three-rings in hopes that speckles of pain
cling to the petroleum and Talc, to Lanolin
or Sorbitan Sesquioleate, to the Beeswax/Cera
Alba/Cire D'Abeille,

Ozokerite,

Mineral Oil/Paraffinum Liquidum/Huile
C12-15 Alkyl Benzoate.

May Contain "+/- CI 77891 (Titanium Dioxide)"
TiO_2 is as fine if it is 100-3,000 nm and ultrafine
if it is smaller than 100 nm.

Findings show that commercial pigments contain
almost no particles smaller than 100 nm.

Scattering of light by TiO_2 is maximized in
particles that are 200-300 nm in diameter.

May Contain Pb, atomic number 82…
…Lead is strongly associated with learning
disabilities and developmental problems.

In fourth grade, he stabs himself in the palm
with a pencil.

In his four-term career the lead
tip still stains his skin. A dot. He shakes hands
and nerves after he speaks of crisis.

A dot connects all. He will mark this day
with stone   Flint. Lead.

Men kiss women, women kiss men
when the center is reached.

METACARTOON

Is it a dream? A junkyard shack? Is it
hey-hey-hey Fat and kids? The T-visions
of wood, loose nails, and a cartoon within
a cartoon? *it's not a bird*, plump and pink;
it's not a bee, old and bearded—white high
tops dangling in space; *it's the Brown Hornet*
and sidekicks destined for disaster, tied
by Dr. Dim's insidious torture:
an out-of-focus-home-movie, white strobes
of Cleveland, syncopated click, cl'k,   cl'k
til the Hornet's mysterious super
powers (snap!) untie the ties and Stinger
and Hornet cheer in outer space. Tune in
next time: Space Ghost's arrest of the Hornet.

WHAT IS THE BROWN HORNET'S KRYPTONITE?

Honey? Found in the dark hollow
of tree trunks or manmade cardboard
box-white hives within hexagon
combs? Unlike bees, Hornet does not
produce honey for consumption.
He does not die when the stinger
inserts his rival foes.
                              Pheromones?
This triggers attack, pointing ass
first, protecting the colony
without fail—death or victory—
the tenacious heroic code.

The Hornet snaps his fingers. Snap!
Stinger free and Tweeterbell safe!
But once more, they fail to refuel.

SPANISH FLY

I suppose I don't know
much about
it.

Perhaps, I tiger-toe in eeny,
meeny,   miny,   moe—
not knowing but knowing.

And I know who hollers
And Mother knows who's
caught in the tiny cotton
fibers knitted into distraction—
an abstract Pollack,
a sweater swirled
of blue and orange,   greens
from forest to lime,   brown
hues throughout.

I suppose when our
Father's duality tears like paper,
his story,   her story,
and the truth in between…

I suppose most, if not all, "heroes"
split their personality,   dual
their nature, secret
their identity,
mask their eyes like children

—peekaboo—

If I can't see
you,

you can't see
me

like emerald beetles crushed
into 0.2-0.7 mg of cantharidin.

Being human with the benefit
of not being human—

Bill Cosby   Brown Hornet

        Bruce Wayne   Batman

Wolverine   James Howlett

        Tony Stark   Iron Man

Green Lantern   Alan Scott

        Scott Summers   Cyclops

Spiderman   Peter Parker

        Matthew Murdock   Daredevil

Incredible Hulk   Bruce Banner

Human without the benefit of
being human—

Batgirl	Pamela Abeyta	
	Jewel Allison	Aquagirl
Batwoman	Janice Baker-Kinney	
	Donna Barrett	Black Cat
Black Widow	Lili Bernard	
	Barbara Bowman	Catwoman
Captain Marvel	Linda Brown	
	Autumn Burns	Echo
Elektra	Sarita Butterfield	
	Renita Chaney Hill	Fallen Angel
Fever	Lisa Christie	
	Andrea Constand	Fire
Ghost	Lachele Covington	
	Janice Dickinson	Grace
Halo	"Dottye"	
	"Elizabeth"	Hawkgirl

Hellcat	Joyce Emmons	
	Beth Ferrier	Huntress
Ice	Carla Ferrigno	
	Charlotte Fox	Invisible Woman
Jade	Tamara Green	
	Chloe Goins	Karma
Killer Frost	Helen Gumpel	
	Helen Hayes	Ladyhawk
Lightning	Colleen Hughes	
	Michelle Hurd	Magma
Maxima	Judy Huth	
	Beverly Johnson	Medusa
Mirage	Kelly Johnson	
	Lisa Jones	Mockingbird
Mystique	Linda Kirkpatrick	
	Cindra Ladd	Night Girl
Nightshade	Chelan Lasha	
	Patricia Leary Steuer	Oracle

Phoenix

Angela Leslie

"Lisa"   Rampage

Raven

Lise-Lotte Lublin

P.J. Masten   Ronin

Secret

Sammie Mays

Katherine McKee   Sepulcher

She-Hulk

Louisa Moritz

Donna Motsinger   Silhouette

Silk

Rebecca Lynn Neal

Linda Ridgeway Whitedeer   Silver Fox

Songbird

Kristina Ruehli

Therese Serignese   Spoiler

Storm

Margie Shapiro

Joan Tarshis   Superwoman

Thunder

Marcella Tate

Heidi Thomas   Venus

Vixen

Jennifer "Kaya" Thompson

Eden Tirl   The Wasp

Wind Dancer   Linda Joy Traitz

                 Shawn Upshaw Brown   Witchfire

Wolfsbane   Victoria Valentino

                 Sharon Van Ert   Wonder Girl

Wonder Woman   Sunni Welles

Human without the benefit of
being human—

"WPA ROAD" OR THE OTHER SIDE OF ETIWAN ISLAND

The men who work on the Etiwan WPA road
project reported for duty as the sun stands.
Thirty-nine negro laborers answered the load.

Their voices ringing out cheerfully in the crowed
air. All of them had long handled shovels in their hands,
the men who work on the Etiwan WPA road.

Some in overalls, some in coats and trousers sewed,
held together by brightly colored patches. They band,
thirty-nine negro laborers answering the load.

Tin buckets and bottles of coffee. A poetic ode
Soon the shovels move rhythmically. Grand,
the men who work on the Etiwan WPA road.

One crew began leveling off humps on the road-
bed. The loose yellow dirt lofted from the fatherland
by thirty-nine negro laborers answering the load.

The sound of soft singing is heard, so low their mode,
so mournful is their song, yet so strong they stand.
The men who work on the Etiwan WPA road.
Thirty-nine negro laborers answering the load.

THE SPIRIT OF DEEP ELLUM

For Blind Lemon

I

He passes his shadow everyday on
his way to and from, where
dark matter still lives and moans—
where a sour pitched voice spiked the skies,
where he blued the guitar, notes
dancing from the rails onto Elm
and Central. Where all tracks connect
to and from the cotton. Have
you ever seen a cotton plant bloom
a lemon—low-hanging fruit?

It's not taboo to fetch the past
for the future.

II

Hank plays at the crossroads on
the days he's not lost in search,
in pursuit for his lineage. He fingers the veins
of his guitar on the same ground
his grandfather once stood. He echoes
country blues, the voice of the people
for the "black downtown," the only place
where religion and hoodooism, gambling
and commerce, theft and law lived on
in chorus without friction.

Hank impersonates his woes, *I ain't got
so many matches but I got so far to go.*

III
From the moment the sun bends
below the horizon through the howl
of the moon, Hank plays the past, calling
upon his ancestors to respond,
calling upon his ancestors to.... They
do not respond. He remains lost
in search. He plucks through pebbles
as if they are Daisy pedals: he loved me,
he loved me not, he loved me, he loved me
not. And so on.

He loved me, he loved me not. He loved
me but soon forgot.

IV
And with each pick, he pictures
an unturned clue in finding his grandfather
as if Lemon is buried under the train's memories,
under the very stones he stood over,
within the ground where his spit
and sweat spilt from his fingers
and whines, where he shared and planted
his soul deep down and dirty, where
Texas heard the imprint of his shoes,
his sole bending the earth's surface.

I stays around Dallas cause I make it there
all the time

V
Hank sifts between alleys, listening to
anecdotes sprouting from the sidewalks
like dandelions: One woman says, "Folks, like honey
bees, swarmed him like he's lemon's nectar;"
another says, "Oh yeah, he'd squeal just

like a dog. Make it sound good, too" Willard
saw him at the Tip-Top dance hall;"
Mance tells Glen, "When we got ta Dallas,
we hung around where we could hear Blind...
It was jest hunnuds a people up an down that Track."

Papa Sollie says, "If they put that money
down heavy, he'd sing heavy."

VI
Hank hides behind the candy shop,
wanting for Truth and Alibi, a chock
house of today, imagined to and from yesterday.
Instead, the candy shop stands as
a hollow home, the headstone for
an empty grave. Here. Now. Lemon blurs
into fluorescents, into neons forming
an open sign. He digs and digs between
Deep's bricks and bones, mortar and tar,
tale and tattle, between here and there.

Hank is not blind,
but he fails to see within.

VII
Could Lemon have rambled at
the R. T. Ashford Record Shop,
409 Central Avenue or the Boyd Hotel, 2934
Elm Street? Sam says, "Jefferson
brought clothes to Model Tailors," 2313
Elm Street, "but seldom sung on Elm."
Could you find him at the Shine
Parlor off 408 North Central or
meandering down Pawnshop Row?
In the end, crumbs fell on Ancestory.com.

Lord, it's one kind favor I'll ask of you.
See that my grave is kept clean.

VIII
Lemon was found in the snow but still
remained lost. His heart broken, froze to
the blister, cold to the world. Hank plays
to the cold almost every day. He plays
to the cold every time. He plays to shake
the spirits of his past awake.

If your heart ain't rock, sugar, must be
marble stone

IX
While looking out, he never looks in.
The treasure buried in his heart and mind,
where X does not mark any spot but dirt.
Hank failed to see. X does not mark the end.
He searched for what he could not be, finding
what he is—the sum of everyone and not just
his grandfather.

His music.
His voice.
His fingers.
His steps.

And for one last time, Hank
slips through Lemon until he becomes,
marking the start.

X
Marks the start.

CHORUS

Nothing you imagine is better than the real.
Being here and now is all you need to feel.

SUSSUDIO SAVES, THE DAY AFTER, #6

01/07/21

The first chance—the five songs
that play in my Silverado on my way
to corral my ten-year-old daughter
from fifth grade:

Living on the Edge by Aerosmith

Eye of the Beholder by Metallica

White, Discussion by Live

Territorial Pissings by Nirvana

Dead Bodies Everywhere by Korn

"There's something wrong…"
rolls on and down the dash
and bounces from the middle console to
weigh my fiber.

Are morals like our first cry from the womb…
innate?

Or are they tweeted…
taught?

Up to the election, I wished for more prescription
drug ads to sober out the political ones—A vote
for Biden is a vote to stand in line for sourdough.

Socialism
or Democracy.

A vote for Trump is a vote to make America great
again.

Fantasy
or Reality.

What does it mean to remake
America…anyway?

Don't we make history by being
present? Don't we make America by being
great? Well, let's save that for another
~~day~~ poem.

Don't you wish political ads had lengthy warnings
like those of the same in prescription ads?
May cause upset stomach, depression, sour
taste in your mouth, and death. Do not take
if allergic to…Do not swallow if pill exceeds
the size of….

But I digress.

"Do you see…" comes
next. I try not to read into it too much; I mean,
my daughter started diagramming sentences
this year. "Dad, where is the direct object?"
she asks. "Dad, is this the simple predicate…is this
a helping verb, and so on?" She identifies
a subject. When all is said and done, the sentence
resembles a tree, branching from the broad

trunk to the specific parts on the leaves. Which
has more depth, the parts or the whole? She
also starts long division this year.

Live sings, "I talk of freedom…"
I don't read into it too much; there's no depth. I mean,
not as if it were really our freedom, as if it were
white hoods on horseback, a hanged black man,
the mother of that man coddling his lifeless body,
his head resting on her bosom like the day he was
born, a mother locking her only son to her breast
for the last time. It's just a song, right?

"…cultures weren't opinions"
plays after. Fantasy or reality? At this point, I need
an escape from the pseudo walls we built. From the
rock and stone that divides us. From the rock and
roll that tells our narrative so well.

Next to show up was *Dead Bodies Everywhere*
by Korn. I cry.

One of my closest friends likes the song,
Whisky in the Jar. Not a bad song, but the
forced rhyme, putting "Oh" at the end
just because "Daddy" and "Jar" don't rhyme.

He's republican. I'm not. He likes *Misery
and Gin*. I like *Drink a Beer*. Don't you see,
differences filter down into song lyrics. It could
be whether you like sad country or drunk country.
It's still music. Red is divided with blue, but
these are just colors. We are still just human beings
with different ears.

Debate
or War.

Truth
or Dare.

Purple is the color of bruises, but it illustrates
healing. But I'm wandering.

"There's this girl that's been…
Su-Sussudio" twists things about.
I remember seeing a banner for Trump saying,
"Stop the Bullshit." I mean, after the election,

after the recounts, Oh
after the courts, Oh
after the rhetoric, Oh
after the anger, Oh
after the insurrection, Oh
after the violence, Oh
after the disappointment, Oh
and, yes,
after all the bullshit, Oh

Sussidio saves me. I can't help but be in awe.
Does art imitate life or does life imitate
Phil Collins?

"BEGGING" OR THERE IS A SHOEMAKER IN THE NEIGHBORHOOD WHO IS WONDERING

Huddled at the door for more,
shoes were full of holes, muddy, cold
fly-specked, weather beaten at the core.

She, the oldest of four
always asking for something to hold,
huddled at the door for more

She stood in line before Pender's Shoe Store,
a thin girl, about fifteen years old
fly-specked, weather beaten at the core.

He always gives away shoes, worn, torn, or
leftovers, the ones he never sold
huddled at the door and nothing more.

One said, "just like poor little rats, begging for
but a biscuit, corn bread, something ignored on the road
fly-specked, weather beaten at the core."

She seemed to have on little, just enough to ignore.
She sure has had a hard time, they told.
Huddled at the door for more
fly-specked, weather beaten at the core.

ISN'T IT?

I hope this doesn't become an Alanis
Morissette song. I still question my
understanding of irony.

BAR GIRL

He's a drunk.
He climps a last drag
the cig strigils orange,
black at its nub.
ashes sprag across his shoes.
Sprag across the floor
like an ongoing novella
lost to the winds,
drenched from the rains
and muddy tire tracks.
Sprag like lifeless poems
circling writer's block,
like jazz notes,
like her legs in my dreams.
She's a dog
She strikes the flint
and hangs the flame under her nose
until the stick catches fire.
She's drunk from the smoke,
drunk from licking the sugar
rim of her martini like a dry hound
sipping puddles of rain and blood
from the bar slugfest
between two pork chops
hounding over her.
He's a drunk.
He roodles through alley scraps,
guddling the tunes, guddling her scent.
The tunes strigil blue:
a *whillywha mizzle* breaths
from the clarinet

a zoozeezaa groans
from the trumpet.
Tap'n his shoes,
he waits to be sucked
up by the notes.
gammerstang to the whiskey,
black at his nub,
he's a downtick
from the booze
and her lipstick kissed glass.
She's a dog.

She bats her lashes,
her daddy's rhizo
in those baby blues.
She has a wamble in her talk
and a jimp jook in her voice.
Jimp jook in her working class collar
starched hard
but trickles silk from the neck down,
I want a little jook in that soda cracker,
a little jimp in that water.

86 THE MUSTARD

The tune floods the whisky
Fingers stain the Scotch

The walls are insomniacs gawking at me—
they hear the same muddle night after night,
Just one more,
their eyes are the florescent beer
signs blinking at me as shuteye
oozes through my veins and inebriates my lids
and my five o'clock whiskers disappear
with my neck tie as last call arrives
and thoughts of hooking up with that brunette piss out,
round the mustard-rimmed Jon
She has quite a pair, but

The toilet takes a piss
The water stinks of Gin

and dreams of being a rock star, a jazz man
some sort of bluez
spill on the floor, guitar strumming
29 songs all at once, a jibber jabber of notes
and growls from the microphone echo in my head
and *oh yeah*
I left Tom in the back room, down to his shoes,
down to a pair of deuces,
playing strip poker but with a switch blade under his toes
in case he wants his clothes back
She has quite a pair

The box playz the last song
A zoobazee blurts out, imitating the sax

The shoes spot blood
and the laces dangle loose outlining a shape—
It seems familiar,
but the symmetric print
from the bottom of my shoe
leaves me to connect the dots but I'm too drunk

Too drunk like the Brunette's lips
and when her tongue flips back forth like a red Robin
flapping its wings over Hollywood
and Vine, my soul sings profanities
because I can't sing
and my zipper seems to be stuck
and that brunette is gone
devil take my soul!
She had quite a pair

The dollar bills lay dead
The shoes fall asleep

and my head limps over the edge
Drown drunk in booze
Drown drunk in love
Drown drunk in drunk
and I lie dead
but my crutch brings me back in
the next night after night

Pour me a Buschmills, Jimmy
Put it on my tab

AT LAST

I told Tony and Mack that it's the third
or second most wedding song. Or something
like that. Her voice cries while in-lovers dance.
The bride howls. He hums. How cd they be so wrong?

I thought it was about love too
until her dream spoke: she follows a rabbit
thru dark groans of soul, a mouse thru mellow zoozeezoos,
thru train songs and storms, thru a kind of Sunday thing.

And thru poppies,
white lines scatter across blue skies,
red is wrapped in clover. *The smell of flowers kill,*
the lion says. Her body deflates while her dream leaks.
Scarecrow scrambles to capture the mist,
anything that clings to straw. The tin man like vanilla,
scoops handfuls into his chest. He's still hollow.

Then I think it's about emptiness.

Then she wakes in the bathroom. Her breasts pressed
against the floor. Her sequined dress loops around
her waist like a belt. Carpet fibers weave thru her hair.

Then I think it's about sex.

But she's alone when she blows the wheeze horn
from last night. And leftover confetti marches out.
The mirror reflects her tiara and then He smiles.
He smiles and heaven is not heaven, it's a metaphor
and her deal that Bob brokered is over.

Then I think it is about finding God.

"EVERY PENNY COUNTS" OR A RELIC OF FORMER DAYS

Housework is never won but always fought.
Mrs. Gray, 57 years old, is a cook and generally
a houseworker. Always too tired to give much thought.

My husband and I, both too old, too taut
to have to work so hard. Her blue eyes weary,
but housework is never won and always fought.

Her straggly light-brown hair all twisted and distraught,
she says, "There's always a job waiting to be."
A houseworker always too tired to give much thought.

"I was born right here in Lawrenceville, and caught
my husband about 38 years ago-I've forgotten when exactly.
Housework is never won but always fought.

We have to do so much to ever get straight, a hardbought
cockfight with the people we owe—so much we need
and always too tired to give much thought.

Her blue dress was almost entirely covered by a white smock
made of bleached muslin. She eased comfortably into a seat
and muttered, "Housework is never won but always fought.
Just a houseworker always too tired to give much thought.

CROSSROADS OF 5TH AND MAIN

"I gotta blow this joint." I say.
The cue ball stinks of spit
and cheap testosterone on shore leave.
Sailors talk drunk and I'm
a sunken ship with an anchor tattoo.

Whites only
Colored round back.

And the boys,
Kenny and Sam pluck chords
behind Daddy's.
Trains rumble through
harmoniz'n the beat.
Hobo Henry blow 'n brass
with his imagination:
fingering empty hands
until his horn is paid from hock.

And ears against Hank William's wall
listen to Blues,
wanting to slip around back
to cross fingers with their bros
and dance in their eyes. Breathe.

But lines aren't crossed.
We only share the music between walls.

While nylon curls and polyester breasts,
Daddy's little girl, hangs her apron
against the register and touches the blue
wall, I ask her to stay one more hour. "For Daddy,
little girl?" I ask.

HOBO HENRY,

his nickname, picked up the trumpet
because, he said, *you don't blow, you don't
get pussy.* When on top, the women guzzled
up his devil sold blues at Daddy's Place,
but now he pisses tunes away for loose
change on the corner of 5th and Main.
He muzzles his horn with a soup can and spats
a few notes in front of the White Only bar,
battling the clangs from the jukebox
and the 1am freight. Cigarette gas filters up
his nostrils and black label jingles his jiggling
cheeks. His yellow eyes squint to the cruel
moonlight, while beads slip over his wrinkled
forehead. His muddy shoes
tap…he does the blues because he must.
And stands at the crossroads willing to sell
his soul. To be on top and plum his cheeks
to the brass and breath the street
each night. It seems like yesterday when I
followed the notes floating in the air, into
the storm drain, into the ears of passers
by reaching their generous hands
as they drop a dollar bill or a nickel into his hat.
And at the end of his set he'd bow to the
empty sidewalk, pocket the money without
counting it, twirl his hat on and disappear
into the dark alley like a ghost caught
in limbo between heaven and hell. Maybe
haunted from the devil, maybe haunted from
the music or just from himself. He slept
in a cardboard box behind Daddy's drinking

his paper bag covered whiskey and howled,
like a mutt, starving for food or waiting
to die. It seems like yesterday, when I found
the words to finish this poem and watch him
die happy, released from his contract
and sent hoboing down the tracks on the 1am
freight headed for the light of day.

GENETIC BLUES

My father hates posing
for photos:
clinch fists
and lips,
Jim Beam yellow
on his teeth,
on his breath.

O, he put the hoodoo in me,
gives me bad luck

I'm a spitting image:
hair slopes,
a crescent moon,
jalopy
without its canopy top.
I spat out profanities.

He put the hoodoo in me,
gives me bad luck

WWW.BLUES.COM

you found it on the net through hard clicking sweat:
a straw fedora brims your sunglasses; a necktie thin
lines your belly.

you found it googlin', popups thrusting
their wisdom on your willin' eyes: an electric
guitar signed by Muddy.

you found it in that old movie pic on showtime.com
in a brown paper bag like a whiskey bottle, a black
gruff-man strapping an acoustic, travelin'
down the rails, tracks tickin' four time.

you bought a package deal, the last minute bid
steals: a silver timepiece dangling down
your pinstripe, Mamie Smith crackling in the background—

That thing called love will make you
sit and sigh
That thing called love...

used to be in the dirt roads, the back alleys,
underground. Down in the Delta, the muggy stew
air, moochin' coin, *I'm worried in my mind.*

used to be in the soul, black nubs
at the cigarette tip, loose strings vibratin'
against loose slides, callus palms and pride
mouthin' their sorrows.

used to be in the corners of the devil's blues, singin'
the sighs of lost loves. *But the best of friends must
part. Now I want somebody please…*

used to be in the woes, and the woo woos
of the nickel train
& not in you, who's me & this poem I wrote.

BLUES ALLEY

I found myself in an alley.
The devil's breath,
as my father's,
overlaps mine.
He whispers sweets
in my ear, tickling spines
on my lobe,
making it hard.

My daughter lay
lifeless by my hands.
A coagulated pool soft
on the asphalt, blue veins
sewn under translucent skin.

A weed
through the cracked street,
barb wire thorns wrap its spine,
making it hard.

"THANK GOD FOR COLUMBUS" OR SAM, THE CANARY

It happens by accident; it's mine. It's artistry—
One day I was shoveling, and I began to sing;
it comes out clear like a canary.

The boys hollered for an encore, they plead.
They don't know no better. Now, I'm Bing.
It happens by accident; it's mine. It's artistry.

My boy is Dennis. So what? We call him Ziggy.
How much waste. A name like Bing,
but it comes out clear like a canary.

Rough laborers, they ain't artistic and touchy
like girls, but they gotta is the only thing—
it happens by accident; it's mine. It's artistry.

They gotta on account of my voice, you see.
That's my nickname in the sewer when I sing.
It comes out clear like a canary.

If a person looks up at the sky and whispers, he's
a Messiah. They depend on this feeling.
It happens by accident; it's mine. It's artistry
that comes out clear like a canary.

CURBSIDE PROPHET

Henry limps into the shop
again, finally flipped from closed.
Heel clicks. Cane taps. He gapes
through the glass counter
and the reflection of his lips
press to the tip of his rusting horn.

"You keep me down
keep me from com'n up." he mumbles.

The owner fiddles his index,
middle, and thumb "You got money?"
he asks. "To hear the rain ting
gainst your brass, again?"

Henry frowns and the glass,
like a funhouse mirror, curves
his face into pear and plum.

"The devil let me down." he says.

And once again, Henry stands
on the corner and his moans, like a crow
cooing its soul, tap the brim
of his hat.

CURBSIDE PROPHET, TOO

I dream up Bob from a poster
stamped on a storefront window.
He is pasted between rhythm
and song.

I dream of avenues,
dumpster cats,
street dogs, warm beer,
and Bob howling steel
sixteenth notes
through the callused nub
of a trumpet stem.

Bob steps into a world of
black.

As dreams fade, I wonder
what the world is
in blue. I dream the world
in a napkin ring
left by the coffee mug filled
with whisky.

DEEP ELLUM'S MIST

I passed him every day.
His sour pitch spiked
the sky. He blued the guitar
neck. I thot: bum.
I thot: no money.
I thot: only debit.
But most of the time
I didn't think at all.

And the last time,
I stepped thru him:

I removed my glasses.
The fluorescents blew
into the street. Faces blurred
neon 'til all was Lemon.
I stood on the corner where black
mist still moaned.

Or was it the next corner?

THE MOON AIN'T ROMANTIC

We continue to share
memories of loss & cigarettes.
They smolder in our lips
staining our stories dull
to everyone else in the bar.

Orange and hiss, flesh
and wind, leave their mark like
needle tracks, like
Mother at the *Blind Pig,* eating
happy hour nuts from a tin bowl
set atop the upright while Tom
growls the indecency of blue.

ZOMBIES

If they could...

if we would
press a voltage meter to their temple, on
through to their rotten-goo-
brain and if it registered,
if it charged,
if those neurons
ramblin in still sparked,
still signaled amongst the village
of others, I think
zombies would
wish for love,
to love, flesh and bone
again, to feel and pulse
again, to imagine
a voice kissing the back of their neck,
hairs stand at attention, polka dots
spring out, up and down their arms
and legs.

After all, they were human
once.

If they could
mold pottery and poetry,
harvest apples and stomp out grapes.

If they could
graft theory from rose stems—
born yellow and purple petals from one bud.

if they could
carve a rib from Adam,
melt steel into sword and create new.

If they could
wield Eve from Adam
and create new on the verge of war
between objects of both sexes
between objects of all sexes,
divided like branches, each branch
new, each bearing fruit dissimilar to
the other—new
If they could,
would we?

After all, we were human
once.

ALBATROSS

I was born to fall, but I try to fly.

"WHEN I AIN'T GOT THAT I DO ANYTHING" OR FRENCHMAN

Drawing noisily at a curved, worn pipe,
he sat in the backyard under an apple tree—
I ain't educated but I can write.

I was a carpenter in Iberville, the east side.
I'm on WPA now. On the brush team.
He says, drawing noisily at a curved, worn pipe,

I learned polishing from an old type,
Italian, I believe. I watched him run the machine.
I ain't educated but I can write.

The first time I tried it, the wheel cried,
running all over the dam stone, free. You see,
drawing noisily at a curved, worn pipe,

I spoiled it. I was fooled. I thought I'd try
and there was nothing to it. But the key
is being educated. At least I can write.

You can't sell granite with a wrinkled tide
in it. But for $2.80 a day, I'll probably flee
And though I ain't educated, I can write,
He repeats, drawing noisily at a curved, worn pipe.

THE INDECENCY OF BLUE

Fire is a woman wearing perfume,
a silkworm emitting pheromones,
a scent, a sense of morphine that numbs
her victims.

The blue base of the fire lingers like
memories of indecency, like needle
tracks, like memories of loss & cigarettes.
It burns to my mouth. I try to remember
her as I try to forget her. But like the ash
that browns my teeth, she will always be
me.

THIS OBSCURE-ORDERING-WOMAN

is a regular, a medium but orders large. "Large cup
with unsweetened Hazelnut Cappuccino with less milk,"
she asks. A cup wanting to overflow with the majority
of her compound, a couple shots of espresso and milk.
Half empty. Less Liquid. Half full. It seems she doesn't
know what fits at all.

DELUXE DOUGHNUTS,

coffee rolls, éclairs, and apple fritters, require their own
transactions. And manager approval. The assistant manager
plays manager when the manager plays apparition, steam
and sugar lift from a large café mocha while his legs
chirp from the desktop. And Gavey counts like day old gravy,
but she makes a mean fountain soda. And the Pakistan girl
mumbles and riots, south central verse Shanila, over the
hassle of one. A just one.

JENGA

He: Just know, you are my world, and I
   will do whatever it takes to make you,
   us, happy

                        She: I will do whatever it takes to
                           make us happy

He: Check out this giant Jell-O shot Jenga

                        She: I LOVE this idea so much! I wish
                           I had this for Friday

He: A bunch of drunk family Tias and Tios
   playing Jenga…pronounced "Henga"
   after one round

                        She: Wendy just bought the jenga game for
                           us. Now I gotta make Jell-o shots!

He: What! How? It said it wouldn't get
   here until after Xmas

                        She: I don't know. We are getting it by Friday.
                           She is good!

He: Wow. Ok.

He: Have the kids make Jell-O shots

He: I think we have Jell-O, too

                    She: I am not sure I trust them with that for my
                            work party but they will handle that for
                            the family one
                    She: We do have Jell-O

                    She: I need a green one for the punch

He: You're so extra

                    She: I get told that on a daily basis

He: Well, if it looks like an orange
        and tastes like an orange, it's an orange

He: I should have said mango

                    She: Yeah. That would have been better

He: Everyone is a critic

JOTO

He insults the cream cheese in Mother's
mother's Christmas pear Jell-O but loves

to string the Douglas Fir with firefly twinkles
like they are gingerbread crumbs from Hansel.

He's lost in song, Bing and Ottis both dreaming
of white. Spiked eggnog loosens the ribbons.

At dinner we chew light and dark a la mode. No
politics or religion, just meat and Jorge's parrot

earring. It dangles from his left ear, an open
invitation to a concealed closet. He died

a little when Papa asked, "¿Donde los encontraste?
Me encantan."

"COONJINE IN MANHATTAN" OR LOVE HER

Here on West Street there is
always a crowding and pushing,
thrusting sharp prows, and a stamping
and stomping,
a romping
of pavement. They seem to toil
with a grim desperation as though the mark
they left was distasteful but necessary.

On this particular day, a gray-haired man
sang, a chanting and a calling,
a refrain in a rhythmical barbaric sort
of regularity—
an inherent love for the beat and
timing of music,
a running back to African days. Coonjine!
Was it possible, I ask.

He awoke longings in my innards:

>   *Love her in de sunshine, Love her in de rain!*
>   *Treats her like a white gal, She give my neck a*
>   *pain!*

In the pocket of his trousers
he clinked one twenty-dollar gold piece
against another. A speckled hen and her
chickens scratch contentedly
in the yard.

It never surfaced through the scratches of

steel and vibration, the *frackled* concrete with spits of raw,
withered grass blades trying to grow where growth
shouldn't happen, through the cracks and veins,
through past and present,
through the soul of a man,

> how whites steal our song,
> steal our face,
> steal,   steal,   steal. He sings

> with in and works with out.

His back bent and the sweat trickled
copiously from his pores, but he would
forget his weariness through song:

> *Do you see that dark cloud risin over yonder?*

> *Do you see that dark cloud risin over yonder?*

> *It's sign of rain, Lord, Lord, it's sign of rain.*

Though the songs fast disappear,
truth to idiom is more important—
Truth to pronunciation, sprinkled
with misspellings:

                                        Ah for I

        Poe for po 1 (poor)
Hit for it
                    Tuh for to
                                        Wuz for was

        Baid for bed
                    Paid for dead
                                        Ouh for our

Mah for my
                                Ovah for over
                Othuh for other
Wha for whar (where)
                                    Undah for under
        Fuh for for
                    Yondah for yonder
                                            Moster for marster
                                            or massa
                Gwainter for gwuieter (going to)
Oman for woman
                                    Ifn for iffen (if)
                Fiuh or fiah for fire
                                        Uz or uv or o' for of
                Poar for poor or po'
                                        J'in for jine
                Coase for cose
Utha for other
                                    Yo' for you
                                    Gi' for give
                                    Cot for caught
                Kin' for kind
                                            Cose for 'cause

Tho't for thought

Whoever wrote "ret" for right is
as accurate as the one who spelled it "raght."

85

PERFECT POEM

This isn't it or do I know
where it is if it exists.
Maybe, the poem lay cold
blue, humming to itself, rejected
from the world, drowning
until muted
by death.

Maybe, it wasn't dead
and vibrates its words
to God, He whispers
them back and
burns them into skin:
a white & black taboo.
Slowly, over time,
it fades grey, lines separate
into lasting imperfections.

Maybe, if the poem exists,
I won't write again,
I would just drink
and be a drunk,
the perfect drunk
to still fuck
and not remember.

REFURBISHED

Susan taught me that poetic energy lies
between the lines, white noise scratching
and clawing between images, ideas,
                                    things...

And like a poem,
the chair was molded by my Tio's hands,
an antique wooden upholstered desk chair.

My Tio moved from Durango, Mexico
to Forth Worth in 1955.

He became a mason and wood worker.

He bricked the stockyards

He built the signs

He died in 2005.

Now,
matted. Worn. Faded floral design. Wood
scarred like healing flesh.

The arms torn, ratted by the heft of his arms
and the stress of the days. The foam peeks
out.

The brass upholstery tacks rusted. I count
1000 of them. With each,
I mallet a fork-tongue driver under its head.

A tap, tap, tapping until it sinks beneath the tack,
until the tack springs from its place.
I couldn't help but think of a woodpecker.
A tap, tap, tapping into Post Oak,
a rhythm…each scrap of wood falling to the ground
until a home is formed.
Until each piece of wood like the tacks removed
shelter something new.

I remove the staples, the foam, the fabric,
the upholstery straps
until it's bones.

I sand and stain
until its bones shine.

I layer and wrap its bones with new upholstery straps,
foam, fabric, staples and tacks.
New tacks, Brass medallions
adorning the whole, but holding it
all together—
its bones
its memories,
its energy.

BLIND SPOTS

My eyes marry the world's
stitches like TV commercials, only
for thirty-second slits, temporary
      inconveniences
in between A Discovery of Witches,
The Handmaid's Tale, Buffy
the Vampire Slayer, or something of
the sort. Only like my introspective
illusions or the unseen—Chevy Impala
on the passenger side, just
outside the corner of my mindset.

According to the driver's education pamphlet,
it is possible to adjust your side
and rear view mirrors to avoid any blind
spots:

> 1776
> *We are determined to foment*
> *a rebellion, and will not hold*
> *ourselves bound by any laws*
> *in which we have no voice*

> 1848
> Seneca Falls Convention

1849
Elizabeth Blackwell becomes—
first female doctor

1869
America's first woman suffrage law
passes in Wyoming

1869
National Woman Suffrage Association
Founded

1916
Margaret Sanger opens first birth
control clinic

1917
Jeannette Rankin becomes—
first woman elected to Congress

1920
the right to vote shall not be denied
or abridged by the United States
or by any State on account of sex

1955
Rosa Parks

1960
Birth control pill

1963
Equal Pay Act

The Feminine Mystique published

Black feminism becomes

1964
Civil Rights Act into law; Title VII
bans employment discrimination
based on race, religion, national
origin or sex

Fat feminism originates

Radical feminism emerges

1966
National Organization for Women becomes

1967
"The Discontent of Women" published

1969
Chicana feminism becomes

1972
Title IX of the Education
Amendments signed

Materialist feminism emerges

1973
Roe v. Wade

1981
Sandra Day O'Connor sworn in—
first woman on the U.S. Supreme Court

The radical lesbian movement

difference feminism develops

equity feminism

1991
Anita Hill testifies

1992
"Becoming the Third Wave"

1994
Violence Against Women Act

Emergence of Riot Grrls

                                    2006
                                    #metoo

2012
Fourth-wave feminism begins

                                    2013
                        Military removes a ban—
                        women serve in combat

2021
Kamala Harris sworn in—
first woman vice president of
the United States

                                    2023
                        Roe v. Wade Reversed

If mirrors are adjusted, blind
spots may not appear; however,
rearward invisibility is entirely
different and requires additional
adjustments.

Notes

Greek Study, Fur Workers, Big Tony, WPA Road, Begging, Every Penny Counts, Thank God for Columbus, When I Ain't Got That I Do Anything

All lines from the U.S. Work Projects Administration, Federal Writers' Project narratives between 1936–39. Some words were altered to fit the poetic form. The quoted titles indicate the title from the original narratives.

Loat and Found

Italicized lines are from the *Ode to a Nightingale* by John Keats

Role Model

Italicized lines from *Dr. Jekyll and Mr. Hyde* by Robert Louis Stevenson

Laid to Rest

Lines are from JFK Testimony, Civil War letters, and student letters

Secret Identity

Italicized lines from *Invisible Man* by Ralph Ellison and *The Rhyme of the Ancient Mariner* by Samuel Taylor Coleridge

The Spirit of Deep Ellum

Italicized lines from Blind Lemon Jefferson

Sussudio Saves, the Day After, #6
Partial lyrics used from the songs *Living on the Edge* by
Aerosmith, *Eye of the Beholder* by Metallica, *White, Discussion* by
Live, *Territorial Pissings* by Nirvana

At Last
Italicized line from *The Wizard of Oz*

www.blues.com
Italicized lines from Mamie Smith's *That Thing Called Love*

Jenga
Text messages between my wife and I days before Christmas

"Coonjine in Manhattan"
Italicized lines and content from the U.S. Work Projects
Administration, Federal Writers' Project narratives between
1936–39. The quoted title indicates the title from the original
Narrative

www.ingramcontent.com/pod-product-compliance
Lightning Source LLC
Chambersburg PA
CBHW070827100426
42813CB00003B/516